Young Learner's

LOOK-n-LEARN

FESTIVALS & CELEBRATIONS

April Fools' Day

April Fools' Day is celebrated on April 1 every year. People carry out various acts of foolishness and play tricks on others. It is also called All Fools' Day.

Ati-Atihan

The Ati-Atihan festival is celebrated in the third week of January in Kalibo on the island of Panay. It honours Santo Niño, the sacred statue of Baby Jesus.

Bakra Eid

Bakra Eid or Eid-ul-Zuha is celebrated by Muslims around the world. On this day, people thank God for their good fortune and give charity to the poor.

Balloon Fiesta

The Albuquerque Balloon Fiesta, held in New Mexico, is the largest hot air balloon festival in the world. Hundreds of hot air balloons are released in the sky.

Bastille Day

Bastille Day is celebrated on July 14 in France. It is a national holiday and is marked with communal meals, music, military parades, dances, etc.

Battle of Oranges

The Battle of Oranges takes place in Italy in February every year. Organised groups throw oranges at each other. It is the biggest food fight.

Calle Ocho

Calle Ocho is a Cuban street festival celebrated in Miami, USA. People gather on the streets and celebrate it with music and food.

Children's Day

Children's Day is celebrated on November 14 in India to mark the birthday of India's first prime minister Jawahar Lal Nehru.

Chinese New Year

Chinese New Year is the biggest holiday in China. It is also known as the Spring Festival and the celebrations last for 15 days.

Christmas

Christmas is celebrated on December 25 as the birthday of Jesus Christ. It is celebrated in a big way with feasts, carol singing, decorating Christmas trees, etc.

Day of the Dead

The Day of the Dead is celebrated in Mexico and other Latin countries on November 1 and 2. On this day, people remember the dead happily and lovingly and carry out many rituals for them.

Desert Festival

The Desert Festival is celebrated in Jaisalmer, India. There are events like camel races and moonlit concerts. The three-day event showcases the land's rich cultural heritage.

Diwali

Diwali is the Indian festival of lights. People decorate their homes with lamps and candles. They light fireworks and exchange gifts.

Dragon Boat

The Dragon Boat festival is celebrated in China to commemorate the death of Chinese patriot Qu Yuan. Teams compete in narrow dragon boat races.

Dussehra

Dussehra is a Hindu festival. It is on this day that Lord Rama defeated and killed the ten-headed demon Ravana. It marks the victory of good over evil. Effigies of Ravana are burnt on this day.

Easter

Easter is celebrated by Christians all over the world. It is believed that on this day, Jesus Christ rose from the dead. People exchange Easter baskets with each other.

Epiphany

Epiphany is celebrated on January 6 every year. It is believed that on this day, the Three Wise Men came to visit Jesus.

Esala Perahera

Esala Perahera is an annual festival held in Kandy, Sri Lanka, to pay homage to the Sacred Tooth Relic of Lord Buddha.

Festival of the Sun

The week-long Festival of the Sun is celebrated in Peru. On June 24, ceremonial events are held in honour of the Sun God.

Glastonbury

Glastonbury is a five-day music festival celebrated in England on the last weekend of June. It also hosts dance, theatre, comedy and other arts.

Grape Throwing

The Grape Throwing festival is held on the last weekend in September in Mallorca, Spain. The festival celebrates the grape harvest.

Guy Fawkes Night

Guy Fawkes Night is celebrated on November 5 in Great Britain. The celebrations include fireworks, a big bonfire and other events.

Halloween

Halloween is celebrated on October 31. Activities like trick-or-treat, ghost tours, bonfires, costume parties, etc. are a part of the celebrations.

Hanukkah

Hanukkah is the Jewish festival of lights. It is observed for eight days by lighting a nine-branch candleholder. Fried foods are eaten during the festival.

Hina Matsuri

Hina Matsuri, also known as Girls' Day, is celebrated in Japan. On this day, people pray for the happiness and health of girls.

Hogmanay

Hogmanay is celebrated on December 31 in Scotland to welcome the new year. Flashy costumes, fireworks and singing are a part of the celebrations.

Holi

Holi is the festival of colours in India. On this day, people throw colours and water at each other. A bonfire is lit on Holi eve to begin the celebrations. Various sweets are prepared on this festival.

Ice and Snow

The Ice and Snow festival is celebrated on January 5 every year in Harbin, China. It lasts for three months. Fireworks, ice sculptures, etc. are its major attractions.

Janmashtami

Janmashtami is celebrated in India as the birthday of Lord Krishna. People make milk products on this day and serve them as an offering.

Junkanoo

Junkanoo is celebrated on December 26 and January 1 in Nassau, Bahamas. It is a street festival that includes music, dance and costumes.

Keene Pumpkin

The Keene Pumpkin festival is celebrated in Keene, USA, in late October. On this day, the Central Square is lined with jack-o'-lanterns kept on every available surface.

Koningsdag

Koningsdag is celebrated on April 26 or 27 in Netherlands as Queen's Day. People gather together and celebrate on the streets with a lot of enthusiasm.

La Tomatina

The La Tomatina festival is celebrated every year in Bunõl, Spain, on the last Wednesday of August. People throw tomatoes at each other for fun.

Las Fallas

Las Fallas is celebrated in Valencia, Spain. There are fireworks and exhibitions on the streets on this day. It is celebrated in March every year.

Mardi Gras

Mardi Gras is celebrated after Epiphany and ends before Lent. Wearing colourful masks and costumes, dancing, parades, etc. are a part of the celebrations.

May Day

May Day is an ancient spring festival and is celebrated on May 1. The celebrations are around a huge striped maypole decorated with flowers and streamers.

Monkey Buffet

The Monkey Buffet festival is celebrated on November 25 in Lopburi, Thailand. Large quantities of fruits and vegetables are given to the local monkeys.

Mother's Day

Mother's Day is celebrated all over the world on the second Sunday of May. Children give gifts to their mothers on this day.

Navratri

Navratri is a nine-day long festival celebrated in India to honour Goddess Durga. People perform pujas and play garba and dandiya during these days.

Navroze

Navroze is the Iranian New Year and signifies the beginning of spring. It is usually celebrated on March 21. Prayers are offered at the fire temple.

New Year's Eve

New Year's Eve parties are held on December 31 with lot of enthusiasm. People party well beyond midnight to welcome the new year.

Obon

Obon is a Buddhist festival and is celebrated in Japan. Families honour the spirits of their ancestors. This festival lasts for three days.

Panafest

Panafest is a cultural celebration held in Ghana. There are various events such as theatre, drama, music, fashion and art. It was first held in 1992.

Passover

Passover is a Jewish festival which is celebrated to mark the liberation of Jewish people from slavery in ancient Egypt.

Pflasterspektakel

Pflasterspektakel is an annual street art festival celebrated in Austria. Juggling, fire dancing and music acts are a part of the celebrations.

Pingxi Lantern

The Pingxi Lantern festival is celebrated in Taiwan. On this day, people release thousands of lanterns carrying messages in the sky.

Purim

Purim is a Jewish festival that is celebrated in March. People make triangular cookies and gift them to each other.

Pushkar

The Pushkar festival is celebrated in Rajasthan, India. It is an annual five-day fair known for its camel fair, exhibitions, music and cultural stalls.

Raksha Bandhan

Raksha Bandhan is celebrated in India. On this day, sisters tie a rakhi around the wrists of their brothers and pray for their long lives.

Ramadan

Ramadan is observed by Muslims around the world as a month of fasting from dawn to sunset. It is considered as one of the Five Pillars of Islam.

San Fermin

The San Fermin festival is held in July in Pamplona, Spain. It features music, folklores, etc. though the main event is running of the bulls.

Sandfest

Sandfest is celebrated in Texas, USA. People gather on the beach at Port Aransas and participate in a sculpture-making competition.

Songkran

The Songkran water festival is celebrated in April as the beginning of the new year in Thailand. It is marked by throwing and sprinkling water on one another.

St. Patrick's Day

St. Patrick's Day is an Irish festival celebrated on March 17. It pays homage to St. Patrick and marks the arrival of Christianity in Ireland.

Tango-no-Sekku

Tango-no-Sekku is celebrated as Boys' Day on May 5 in Japan. Young boys display miniature warriors, suits of armour, swords, bows and arrows, etc.

Thanksgiving Day

Thanksgiving Day is celebrated in USA on the fourth Thursday of November and in Canada, on the second Monday of October. It includes a grand turkey dinner.

Tomorrowland

Tomorrowland is an electronic dance music festival held at the end of July every year in Belgium. It is one of the most notable global music festivals.

Trung Thu

Trung Thu is a children's festival celebrated on a full moon day in August in Vietnam. Children feast on moon cakes filled with sugar and meat.

Veterans' Day

Veterans' Day celebrates people who have served in the U.S. Armed Forces. It is celebrated on November 11.

White Nights

The White Nights festival is celebrated in June in Russia with fireworks, concerts and a mock pirate battle.